Helen Herron Taft

Helen Herron Taft

1861–1943

By Judith E. Greenberg

CHILDREN'S PRESS®
A Division of Grolier Publishing
New York   London   Hong Kong   Sydney
Danbury, Connecticut

To Anita Kallfelz for her friendship and the use of her escape garden

Acknowledgments: Thank you to Priscilla Thompson for her Cincinnati research and to Dalia Amir for her joyous help.

Consultant: LINDA CORNWELL
                Coordinator of School Quality and Professional Improvement
                Indiana State Teachers Association

Project Editor: DOWNING PUBLISHING SERVICES
Page Layout: CAROLE DESNOES
Photo Researcher: JAN IZZO

Visit Children's Press on the Internet at:
http://publishing.grolier.com

Library of Congress Cataloging-in-Publication Data
Greenberg, Judith E.
        Helen Herron Taft, 1861–1943 / by Judith E. Greenberg
            p. cm. — (Encyclopedia of first ladies)
        Includes bibliographical references and index.
        Summary: A biography of the wife of the twenty-seventh president of the United States, an ambitious woman who was responsible for planting the famous cherry trees around the Tidal Basin.
        ISBN 0-516-20643-5
        1. Taft, Helen Herron, 1861–1943—Juvenile literature. 2. Presidents' spouses—United States—Biography—Juvenile literature. [1. Taft, Helen Herron, 1861–1943 2. First ladies. 3. Women—Biography.] I. Title II. Series
E762.1.G74   2000
973.91'2'092—dc 21   99-33423
[B]   CIP
                                                        AC

Table of Contents

Helen Herron Taft

CHAPTER ONE

Early Memories

* * * * * * * * * * * * * * * * *

Helen Herron Taft was a very interesting and politically aware woman of her day. She grew up just after the American Civil War, even telling people a story of sitting on the front steps of her house and watching a parade. Too young to understand it then, Helen later realized it was a peace celebration for the close of the Civil War.

Growing up in the mid-1800s in Cincinnati, Ohio, left Helen (nicknamed Nellie) Taft with many fond memories. She freely admitted that it was a dirty, noisy, and polluted city. It was also an important one because it was on the direct route from the East to the West.

* * * * * * * * * * * * * * * * *

Cincinnati as it looked about 1872, when Helen lived there with her family

A view of Cincinnati as it looked from the Carlisle Hotel in the 1800s

Much of Cincinnati's growth in the early 1800s resulted from Ohio River trade.

Portrait of America, 1861: Two Americas

✫ ✫

Upheaval and uncertainty marked the year that Helen Herron was born. Slavery and other disagreements tore the country apart. By 1861, 11 Southern states had seceded from the Union to form the Confederate States of America. That left 23 states, including far-flung California and Oregon, and 23 million people in the North. The 11-state Confederacy included nearly 9 million people, about 3.5 million of whom were black slaves. A civil war between the two Americas would begin and last four bloody years. The first shots were fired on Fort Sumter in Charleston, South Carolina, on April 12, 1861.

Two presidents ruled over the divided nation. In the North, Abraham Lincoln was inaugurated as the sixteenth president of the Union. Just weeks before, Jefferson Davis had been sworn in as president of the Confederate states. Neither man could have imagined what lay ahead. Thinking the conflict could be ended quickly, Lincoln asked for 75,000 volunteers to enlist for three months. By the actual end of the war four years later, an estimated 2 million Northern soldiers had served.

Americans got their first taste of the terrible war to come on July 21 at the First Battle of Bull Run fought at Manassas Junction just outside of Washington, D.C. So confident were Northern supporters that many civilians drove out from the city with picnic lunches to watch the fight. They witnessed a frightening defeat. After the bloodshed, fleeing soldiers and carriages filled with terrified sightseers clogged the muddy roads back to the capital. Clearly, victory in this war would be difficult and costly.

While the South slipped away, many Americans were pushing west. By 1861, the frontier—that imaginary boundary between civilization and wilderness—lay just about down the middle of the continent from the western edge of Lake Superior to the southern tip of Texas. Kansas joined the Union as the newest free state, and the territories of Dakota, Colorado, and Nevada were organized. For the first time, 3,500 miles (5,633 kilometers) of telegraph line, called "Lightning Wire," connected the East and West Coasts, eliminating the need for mail delivery by Pony Express.

While North and South prepared for war, Yale University awarded its first Ph.D. degree. Eccentric Matthew Vassar donated money he had made brewing beer and a little land to establish Vassar Female College in Poughkeepsie, New York. Thaddeus Lowe journeyed a record 900 miles (1,448 km) in a balloon, and the first pretzel factory opened in Pennsylvania. Patents were issued for 2,919 new inventions.

Though divided, the American spirit seems not to have dimmed.

All seats were filled at the opening symphony concert at Cincinnati's Exposition Hall.

Both Helen's and William's fathers belonged to the Literary Club of Cincinnati (above).

Many Germans settled in the city and started symphonies, music groups, and book clubs. Both Helen's father and Willliam Taft's father belonged to the Literary Club of Cincinnati. Helen's father, uncle, and two brothers were all college graduates, and she enjoyed growing up in an atmosphere of intellectual traditions.

Helen attended a girls' school, Miss Nourse's School, which the girls nicknamed the "Nursery." Besides learning languages and literature, she spent much of each day practicing the piano. She had a lifelong passion for music.

Raising Helen and her brothers and sisters was not an easy task, espe-

While at Miss Nourse's School, Helen spent much of each day practicing the piano.

cially as there were a total of eleven Herron children. Helen was the fourth child of eight girls and three boys. Two girls and one boy died before Helen could even remember them. The rest survived and had to be fed and cared for. Helen's father, a lawyer and a state senator, earned a decent income but always had to be concerned about feeding and educating his large family. During this time in the United States, very large families were not unusual. Helen's popular mother was always busy with the children and ran a happy house.

A very special teenage memory involves Helen and First Lady Lucy Hayes. The adult Herrons and the

13

A scene at the White House when the Grants left after Rutherford B. Hayes was elected president

A visit to the White House with President Rutherford B. Hayes (below) and his wife Lucy (above) was a highlight of Helen's life.

Hayeses had been lifelong friends. Rutherford B. Hayes had been a partner in Helen's father's law firm before becoming president. Helen's younger sister was born shortly after the Hayeses came to the White House. She was named Lucy Hayes Herron after the First Lady. The baby was even christened at the White House. When Helen was seventeen years old, she was invited—along with her sister and her sister's husband—to stay at the White House for a week. Helen recalled the thrill of going to Washington, D.C., for the first time and the delight at being a guest in the White House. She remembered that the Hayeses lived very quietly. Helen spent most of her time like any other

Washington, D.C., tourist, seeing the sights of the capital city.

A year later, Helen met William Howard Taft, or Will, as she called him. Although they had lived in the same town, grown up with several of the same friends, and had fathers and mothers who knew one another well, Will and Helen didn't really know each other. The Tafts lived in a suburb of Cincinnati, and Will left for Yale right after high school. There were very few times that Helen's and Will's paths might have crossed and given them an opportunity to meet. They finally did meet one winter night at a

Will and Helen finally met at a sledding party with a group of friends.

William Howard Taft went to college at Yale right after high school.

sledding party. Will was introduced to Helen and offered to take her down the hill on his bobsled. After that, they were together more often as they were part of a group of friends who attended amateur theater productions. They also had parties in the country-side on the banks of the Ohio River.

While enjoying all these outings with Helen and his friends, Will still worked hard at his career. He was a law reporter and later practiced law with a man who had been a partner of Taft's father. It was around this time that Helen also decided that parties couldn't be her whole life. She took a

15

Helen began teaching piano at a private school when she was nineteen.

Helen preferred reading books and playing the piano to formal dances.

job teaching in a private school. Helen was a bright and outstanding student, so it was no surprise that she turned to teaching, especially teaching piano. Helen was never as attractive as her sisters, and she knew this. She even wrote in her diary about her strong ambitions, her discontent, and her literary tastes. She wrote that she wanted to be loved but could only imagine loving a man who considered her his intellectual equal. By the time she was nineteen, she wanted very much to write a book and preferred music and books to ball

gowns. She became shy and quiet when young men were around. Nellie withdrew deeper into herself as she watched her friends marry, one by one.

Fortunately, William Taft saw a different person when he was with Nellie. While they were as different in nature as they were in size, he liked her quiet strength. She was slim and active, with a tiny waist, dark hair, and a stubborn mouth and chin. Pic-

Nellie (second from left, front) organized this literary club in the 1880s. Will Taft is next to her.

tures of Helen Taft taken from her teens through the White House years show that she changed very little. She was small and well built with an attractive but not gorgeous face. It was her way of holding herself that showed her strength and intelligence and created her beauty. She always dressed well even though shopping was not of much interest to her.

Time passed as Will and Nellie grew to know each other and to work on their careers. For a time, both dated other people. Helen even had dinner and drank wine with an escort at a restaurant. This was considered very racy for her time. Lighting a cigarette in public was also considered

"fast" behavior for a lady, but Helen did that, too. She had a few serious suitors, or men who wanted to marry her, but she seems to have been interested only in Will and one other young man. The thought that she might choose the other man truly upset Will, and he set out to win her.

Both families hoped for the marriage, but no one would push Nellie into anything unless her mind was made up and she really wanted it. Will had to do all the work himself. And work hard he did. When he first asked her to marry him, she told him she'd have to think about it.

His involvement in political activities and writing articles for newspapers about clean politics kept Will busy while Helen Herron was making up her mind. Even Will's father wrote to him and urged Will to make their plans public. Nellie often felt insecure about marrying Will as she felt that he couldn't love such a plain girl. Sometimes she was very moody, but Will still loved her.

Will was offered the position of assistant county solicitor and received $2,500 a year for the job. This allowed

Keeping Fit—Nineteenth-Century Style

★ ★

You probably know someone who goes to a health club to do aerobics and pump iron. How about someone who goes to a gymnasium to do calisthenics and lift dumbbells? Probably not, although a century ago, many Americans kept fit by doing just that. Indeed, around the middle of the 1800s, the nation went crazy for fitness. As the country became more urban and industrialized, people began to work more at office jobs than outside at farming and other tasks requiring physical labor. Americans felt the effects of this increase in "brain work"—as desk jobs were often called—as a decrease in their good physical health. At the same time, new German immigrants to the United States inspired Americans, especially in the Midwest, with their organized approach to physical fitness. Physical-education classes in schools became popular. For adults, public gymnasiums offered classes in calisthenics—rhythmic body exercises sometimes performed to music. They also provided exercise equipment such as rowing machines and other devices remarkably similar to those we use today, along with apparatus for gymnastic activities such as ropes for climbing and parallel bars. Hand-held wooden dumbbells helped increase muscle and joint flexibility, and "Indian clubs" shaped like bowling pins were swung around in certain patterns to shape and tone the upper body. Women were encouraged to participate in the exercise craze, but only if properly attired, of course, in baggy, full-cover gym suits.

Will to feel comfortable enough to try again to persuade Helen to marry him. They became engaged in May 1885. Helen's wedding dress was made in Washington, D.C. She cried when she first saw herself in it as she believed she looked quite ugly.

Wedding presents started to arrive and Will and Nellie were constantly together. They went roller skating, to dog shows, and even worked out with dumbbells due to her touch of rheumatism. Many days were spent taking the morning streetcar to the

During their engagement, Will and Nellie often went roller skating (left). They spent the summer enjoying the fresh air and exercise in the Adirondacks (center and right) with Helen's family.

Helen Herron in the dress she wore when she married William Howard Taft on June 19, 1886

site of their future home on McMillan Street. The property had been a wedding present from Helen's father. The summer of their engagement was spent in the Adirondacks (mountains) enjoying a lot of healthy air and exercise with the rest of Helen's family. That winter, they were kept busy planning the house they would build. On June 19, 1886, when Will was twenty-nine and Nellie was twenty-five, they married in her family's home.

Helen and Will traveled to Europe for their wedding trip, or honeymoon. It was Helen's first trip to Europe. The

19

Woman or Sofa?

★ ★

As Helen Taft well knew, Paris was the undisputed capital of fashion in the 1880s. French designers dictated fashion trends, and expensive dressmakers created elegant garments for their wealthy clients. Elite Americans who could afford the trip returned from Paris with a full season's wardrobe. And what a wardrobe! Women's dresses of the 1880s were renowned for their complexity. Intricate dressmaking and luxurious materials went into expensive gowns that reflected their wearer's status and wealth. Obviously unsuitable for work, these draped and layered ensembles set the lady of leisure apart. The most elaborate gowns called for yards and yards of costly fabric to drape and pad the wearer's figure. They often incorporated both a plain and a patterned material that blended rich colors and the various textures of silk, velvet, and wool. If that weren't enough, ribbons, lace, and beaded or fur trims added just the right finishing touch. Under it all, the fashionable lady wore a tight corset to diminish her waist and, at her back, a frame called a bustle to accentuate her posterior. Indeed, draped, layered, and padded, the best-dressed woman of the 1880s closely resembled a piece of upholstered furniture.

boat trip across the ocean went smoothly. The couple spent most of the summer in England and then visited Holland and Paris. The trip lasted one hundred days and cost $1,000! While in Paris, Helen had three outfits made by French dressmakers. Originally, she was frightened to death of going to Parisian dressmakers, thinking they would find her unworthy of their creations. But in true Helen Herron Taft style, she marched ahead and had them make a brown silk reception dress, a rose silk dinner dress, and a green cashmere dress that Will was especially fond of as it fit her so well. Even after spending money on the dressmakers, Helen insisted on riding buses while sightseeing rather than taking carriages, as she hoped it would save them some money for more sightseeing.

Deck quoits was a popular pastime during ocean crossings between the United States and Europe.

Piccadilly Circus (an intersection in London) as it looked when the Tafts were there in 1886

William Howard Taft as a judge of the Superior Court of Ohio

Once they arrived home, they set up housekeeping. Will was a very happy man. He was appointed a judge of the Superior Court of Ohio with a salary of $6,000 and was elected again for five years. This work did not take him away from home and his bride who suited him so very well. Nellie realized that Will's chances for national power were great, and she helped him guide his career in the direction she wanted it to go.

21

The baby in the carriage in front of the Tafts' house on McMillan Street is probably Robert.

Nellie with her first two children, Robert, at the age of two (right), and Helen, six months old

In 1889, on September 8, the first child of Will and Nellie Taft was born in their home on McMillan Street. He weighed 8 pounds (3.6 kilograms) and was named Robert. Will Taft was the happiest man alive!

Little Robert was not an easy baby. He was always hungry, and as a toddler, he ran around with the energy of ten boys. Once, he even covered himself with shoe polish! As he grew, he did settle down until the arrival of his baby sister, Helen, on August 1, 1891. Robert is said to have been upset and shouted "more baby!" For a while, everyone called the new girl "more baby" and sometimes "Helen Blazes," as she often screamed and cried.

Will's reputation as a judge was continuing to grow, and he had an important reputation as a lawyer for cases involving big business, railroads, and labor unions. He was now a circuit court judge, which meant he rode from area to area to sit as judge for each of those communities and counties. As a circuit court judge, he made many firm, sometimes unpopular, rulings. To relax, the Tafts would go to Murray Bay on the St. Lawrence River in Canada and stay in a small, modest cottage. They always enjoyed this riverside getaway and eventually

William Howard Taft with his children—Helen (on his knee) and Robert

A colored drawing of Judge Taft at the time he and Theodore Roosevelt became friends

stayed in hotels rather than a small cottage.

The third and last of their children, Charles, was born on September 20, 1897. Helen continued her chores as mother to three small children while her husband was riding the circuit as a judge. Nellie poured much of her own energy into inspiring her three children toward her own high ideals, love of music, and enthusiasm for new experiences. She also organized and ran the Cincinnati Orchestra Association.

Will was meeting many important people and caught the eye of others who would later be of special importance to him and his family. He was beginning to be known on a national and international level. His father wrote to him often of his pride in his son. Even Theodore Roosevelt was hearing of Taft. The two men would soon have a special friendship.

CHAPTER TWO

The Philippines

Because Helen Taft loved travel and adventure, when Will came home one day and told her he had been offered a new position by President McKinley, she was thrilled. "Take it," Helen said, and so did Will's brothers. The job was not one that Will really wanted, nor was he very fond of President McKinley. This job would require that Will give up his circuit court judgeship and go to the Philippine Islands. There, he would act as head of a commission that was to establish a peaceful civilian government. Will had not approved of the Spanish-American War and wasn't very thrilled with the idea of going to the

President McKinley appointed Taft head of a commission to establish a government in the Philippines.

Taft (center) with Luke Wright (left) and Henry Ide, members of the Philippine commission

Philippines, islands that the United States had received after the war. The president made Will realize that he was needed in this post as he had a good sense of people and was known to be fair and honest. Nellie said she knew "instantly that I didn't want to miss a big and novel experience."

After all the discussions and planning, the whole family left for the Philippines. Helen had been told that it would be best to leave her children at home to keep them safe from any diseases they might catch in the Philippines. But she didn't want to break up the family and certainly wouldn't have missed the chance to go herself. Also, as a person who loved learning and adventure, she wanted her children to have as many unusual and wonderful experiences as possible. The children were ten, eight, and two

The Spanish-American War: Fast Facts

WHAT: The Cuban war for independence from Spain

WHEN: Cuba had struggled for independence since the Ten Years' War of 1868 to 1878. Open revolt again broke out in 1895.

WHO: Cubans rebelled against their Spanish rulers. The United States entered the conflict in 1898 after the U.S. battleship *Maine* blew up in Havana Harbor.

WHERE: U.S. troops fought the Spanish in naval and land battles in Cuba and the Philippines. At war's end, U.S. troops captured the Spanish colony of Puerto Rico.

WHY: The Cubans rebelled against Spanish rule. Americans clamored for military intervention, especially after the loss of the *Maine* with more than 260 American lives. Many Americans saw war with Spain as a way for the United States to become a world power.

OUTCOME: The war lasted ten months. The U.S. victory had been relatively easy, but not without cost. While 385 men were killed in action, more than 5,100 died of disease and accident. The peace treaty granted Cuba its independence, and the United States received Puerto Rico, Guam, and the Philippines from Spain.

Honolulu, Hawaii, as it looked about the time the Tafts arrived in 1900

Helen and the Taft children stayed in Japan for a time, while Will and the other members of the commission continued their journey to the Philippines.

The emperor and empress of Japan, shown here in their state carriage, received Will and Helen Taft when they arrived in Japan.

when their home was sold, their furniture put in storage, and they boarded the army transport *Hancock*. It was April 17, 1900.

The whole family enjoyed the smooth crossing, and Helen was proud of the fact that her oldest son beat nearly everyone at chess. Landing first in Honolulu, Hawaii, the family learned of many delights including surfing, leis, and luaus. From Hawaii, they went on to Japan, where Mr. and Mrs. Taft were received by the emperor and empress of Japan. While

Will and the members of the commission continued their journey, Helen and the children stayed for a while in Japan. They fell ill one at a time, and for a while, someone in the family was either in the hospital or in quarantine. They also survived earthquakes and a brutal rainstorm. These setbacks did not stop them from visiting lovely gardens and beautiful Japanese stores.

The Philippines is an island country in the southwest Pacific Ocean. It is made up of 7,000 islands, but the 11 largest are the main part of the coun-

The Escolta—the principal thoroughfare of Manila—as it looked when the Tafts were there

Thick tropical forests like this one cover most of the Philippine islands.

The town of El Nido on Palawan Island has Bacuit Bay at its front and mountains at its back.

try. The capital city is Manila. The people of the Philippines are called Filipinos. Many of the people are dark-haired and dark-skinned and speak both Spanish and English. In 1898, Spain gave the Philippines to the United States as part of the treaty that ended the Spanish-American War. The United States would rule the island nation until 1935. Today, the population is made up mainly of Filipinos—most of whom are related to the Malays of Indonesia and Malaysia—and Chinese. Smaller numbers of Americans, Europeans,

Indians, and Japanese also live in the Philippines. The two official languages are English and Pilipino, which is a variation of Tagalog and is based on Malay languages.

Thick, tropical forests cover most of the Philippines and active volcanic mountains rise up from most of the islands. There are many fine bays and harbors, and a wide variety of plants and animals are found there. Caribou, an animal like a water buffalo, as well as tropical birds, monkeys, snakes, and crocodiles are found in the islands. The climate is hot and humid with about 100 inches (254 centimeters) of rain per year. When the Tafts were there, they endured the heat and humidity with the help of many household servants who did the difficult jobs so Nellie and her children could enjoy the country but not overwork themselves in the tropical heat.

While the family was enjoying their adventures in Japan, Will was setting up his office in the Philippines and having a very dreary house repaired. In her autobiography, Mrs. Taft talks about the big house and the bay that was right behind them. She de-scribes how Will kept trying to keep a sea wall up to protect the children from getting into the bay. However, every time the rains came, parts of the wall went! The house was big and roomy with a glassed-in porch that ran the whole length of the house and faced the bay. Mr. Taft had electric fans put in the house to help cool the tropical air. When there was a typhoon, the whole house rattled and shook so much it seemed as if it might fall to pieces.

The military governor of the islands was Major General Arthur Mac-Arthur. He treated the Tafts with little kindness. He resented the commission that had come to establish civil government. Taft went about his business of helping the Filipinos to have a say in their government and began to enjoy the beauty of the country as well as the friendliness of the people. Because the army was still segregated, it was not general policy for MacArthur or other officers to invite any Filipinos to dinner or as guests in army quarters. When Mrs. Taft arrived with her children in the summertime, she set about breaking down that barrier. She gave a

Arthur MacArthur, Jr. (1845–1912)

✫ ✫ ✫ ✫ ✫ ✫ ✫ ✫ ✫ ✫ ✫ ✫ ✫ ✫ ✫ ✫ ✫ ✫ ✫ ✫

Arthur MacArthur was the father of one of America's most famous fighting men, General Douglas MacArthur. Arthur himself lived an impressive military life as well, and the MacArthurs are the only father and son to receive Medals of Honor for "uncommon valor." Living in Wisconsin at the outbreak of the Civil War in 1861, the teenaged Arthur enlisted with the 24th Wisconsin Volunteer Infantry. He distinguished himself at Missionary Ridge, Tennessee, in 1863, where, though wounded, he raised the regimental flag in the heat of battle. When the Civil War

ended, Arthur studied law, but soon returned to the army, where he spent the rest of his career. After the Spanish-American War, President McKinley named him the military governor of the Philippines. Stubbornly resisting William Taft's civilian authority there, MacArthur was transferred back to the United States. He retired from the army as a lieutenant general in 1909. Five years later, MacArthur was invited to address a reunion of the 24th Wisconsin, attended by ninety of his aged Civil War comrades. During the presentation, the general suffered a massive heart attack and died. His fellow soldiers solemnly wrapped MacArthur in the remains of the old battle flag he had carried to the top of Missionary Ridge. A lifelong wish granted, Arthur MacArthur had died at the head of his regiment.

party for General MacArthur with a band and charming decorations all over the huge house. She also invited Filipinos. Gradually, Helen and Will were able to break through the color barrier.

Though the Taft children had little understanding of what their father was doing, they very much enjoyed living in the Philippines. They had ponies to ride, trees to climb, monkeys to watch, kites to fly, and friends who spoke

General Arthur MacArthur (second from left) with some of his staff in the Philippines

Will and Nellie Taft with their son Charlie in the Philippines

33

Spanish and helped the Taft children learn the language and customs. Their education was unstructured and came from learning about the country and its people. Eventually, the children attended a school set up to help the Filipinos develop and improve their school system. Life at home, however, was fairly simple and easygoing. The family's cook kept them all well fed with such things as mangoes and banana fritters, lobsters and shrimp. Will Taft had always been a large man, and he now began putting on even more weight. A bathtub big enough for him was put in the house.

The whole family went along on a trip through sixteen Filipino provinces in 1901. Taft worked very hard, holding meetings and helping to set up government in each place they visited. He helped establish local officials, and Filipino governors were chosen wherever possible. By April, Taft was beginning to feel the strain of his job and the added strain of the tropical weather. He had worked for many hours every day and didn't rest, something that is not a good idea in the tropics. Even though he felt the

strain, he worked on and was sworn into office as the first civil governor of the Philippines on July 4, 1901. General MacArthur left, and the Tafts moved into his house, which was called Malacanan Palace. Even though it was called a palace, it wasn't much like one. The mosquitoes drove the family crazy all the time. There were about twenty rooms and a wonderful roofless porch that allowed the night breezes to cool them. The house, larger than their other one, required more servants. It took six servants just to keep the floors polished. They tied banana leaves to their feet

Mount Mayon, a volcano on Luzon, the largest Philippine island

William Howard Taft (far right, back row), Nellie (third from left, back row), Charlie (center, back row), and other associates with Filipino children during the time Taft was civil governor of the Philippines

A street in the Philippine village of Cavite as it looked when the Tafts were there

Moro huts on the banks of the Rio Grande del Mindanao

35

This cartoon was published at the time Taft became governor of the Philippines.

The Tafts moved into Malacanan Palace when General MacArthur left the Philippines.

and skated back and forth until the floor was shiny and slippery. Then they went into another room and started all over again.

The salary that went with being governor of the Philippines was an amazing $25,000. At first, the Tafts thought they were rich! But in reality, they had to use so much of this money to entertain and keep up the appearance of the governor's house, that it was never enough. As governor, Taft's duties were still very much the same as when he headed the commission, but the new title brought a great deal of prestige to his work. Mrs. Taft gave afternoon receptions once a week. Announcements of receptions were published in the newspaper.

For three terrifically exciting years, the Taft family lived in the Philippines. During that time, they traveled as many miles as two trips around the world! Mrs. Taft and her sister once took a donkey trip up into the mountains and finally came to a hotel where they spent time relaxing and enjoying the social life.

To get around on the island, Nellie had a matched set of black ponies and

Governor Taft and Mrs. Taft with their children and others in Venetian Carnival costumes, 1903

This photograph of Charlie Taft was taken when he lived in the Philippines.

a carriage that could be drawn by the little horses. These horses were quite small but strong and fast. They moved quickly through traffic and seemed to almost crash with every turn in the road. Once when the children were out in the carriage, Charlie, the youngest Taft, was thrown under the carriage and the wheels went over him. After the excitement died down, Charlie was fine, but Nellie rarely let them go out without proper adult care again. Mr. Taft had his own ponies to take his carriage to the office and back each day. Because there was very little public transportation, the ponies be-

The Assassination of President McKinley

☆ ☆

William McKinley was the third American president to fall to an assassin's bullet after Abraham Lincoln and James Garfield. At the time of his death, Americans were looking forward to a promising new century with President McKinley at the

helm for his second term. It was September 6, 1901, and the president was attending the Pan American Exposition, a grand fair of trade and invention in Buffalo, New York. McKinley reached to shake hands with a young man, who offered not his hand but a loaded pistol in return. Doctors treated McKinley for eight days with a diet of "whiskey, water, and raw eggs," but were unable to find or remove the bullets from his stomach. Gangrene soon set in and McKinley died on the eighth day. Ironically, though a newfangled "X-ray" machine was on display at the exposition, McKinley's doctors never used it to examine him. The assassin, an unemployed twenty-eight-year-old steel worker by the name of Leon Czolgosz, was speedily convicted and sent to the electric chair.

came very important and were well cared for by the stable boys.

Working daily to try to complete his job as head of the commission and then as governor, Taft spent time debating or investigating or listening to others about all that needed to be done in the Philippines. So many problems existed that it seemed like too much to finish, but Taft worked on. The commission dealt with issues such as taxation, currency, police, harbor improvements, roads and railways, postal service, schools, health, hospitals, church lands, honest judges, fair laws, and the immediate need to help the people realize that they were really at peace. It was a staggering workload, one that had to go on even after President McKinley was shot by an assassin in September 1901. His death was a staggering blow to the commission, yet they continued their work.

Taft's work was cut short when he suffered an illness that required two operations. The new president, Theodore Roosevelt, felt it was time for the Tafts to leave the tropics for a while. They left on Christmas Eve 1901. Nellie Taft had suffered from the strain of being the governor's wife. In addition, she had to deal with her husband's illness and the news that her mother at home was seriously ill. All these burdens caused Helen herself to fall ill. When they finally reached Cincinnati, it was just in time for her mother's funeral, but Nellie was too ill to attend. It took two months for her to recover. Will went on to Washington, D.C., to consult with President Roosevelt before returning to the Philippines.

☆　☆　☆　☆　☆　☆　☆　☆　☆　☆　☆　☆　☆　☆

CHAPTER THREE

A Career in the Capital

☆ ☆ ☆ ☆ ☆ ☆ ☆ ☆ ☆ ☆ ☆ ☆ ☆ ☆ ☆

Washington, D.C., is like a magnet for anyone who wants to serve his or her country. Because this city on the Potomac River draws people who want the power of top elected positions, many politicians get "Potomac Fever." William Howard Taft was not this sort of man. He believed in public service as an honor and a duty. He did not really want to run for president—his dream was to be the chief justice of the Supreme Court. Helen Herron Taft, however, had other ideas. From the time she was a young woman of seventeen and visited President and Mrs. Hayes in the White House, Helen had "Potomac Fever." She was

☆ ☆ ☆ ☆ ☆ ☆ ☆ ☆ ☆ ☆ ☆ ☆ ☆ ☆ ☆

William Howard Taft was appointed secretary of war by President Theodore Roosevelt.

Secretary of War Taft (left) with the engineers responsible for the construction of the Panama Canal

President Theodore Roosevelt (in high-backed chair against the doors) with his cabinet, which included Secretary of War William Howard Taft (far left)

determined to help her husband become president.

One step along the way to that dream was for Will to have a career in Washington, D.C. He was already well known and respected for his good work in the Philippines, and now she felt it was time for him to gain more fame and recognition. In 1904, after the resignation of Elihu Root, Taft became President Theodore Roosevelt's secretary of war. Roosevelt and Taft were good friends and worked well together. The president depended on Will to take care of many rough situations during the next few years.

Taft's department supervised the construction of the Panama Canal.

Construction of the Panama Canal

Charlie Taft, Helen and Will's youngest son, playing quoits on the deck of an ocean liner

President Roosevelt's daughter Alice (center front) accompanied the Taft party when the group went to the Philippines to open the Legislative Assembly.

This canal would join the Atlantic and Pacific Oceans and make both travel and shipping easier and faster. An article in the *New York Sun* praising Taft's work made Helen very proud. In part, it said, "Merely to record the movements and missions of the secretary of war requires a nimble mind. He journeys from Washington to . . . Panama to speed the digging of the . . . Canal."

In 1906, Taft was sent to Cuba to

In 1906, Taft was sent to Cuba to help negotiate peace when it appeared there would be a revolution. When Helen pulled into Havana Harbor (above) to join her husband, she was greeted by a gun salute.

help negotiate peace when revolution threatened. In only eight days, Taft got things under control without a single gun being fired. The U. S. Marines had already been ordered to go to Havana, Cuba, and Helen went with them to join her husband. Because many Cubans wanted to become part of the United States, Mrs. Taft pulled into the harbor to the sound of a gun salute. Ships dipped their flags in her honor, and once again she was treated like the First Lady she so wanted to be. She soon managed the task of getting herself and Will home.

The problems with Cuba came up again two years later when the government there started to fail again. Cuba's president, Tomás Estrada Palma, worried that innocent people would be hurt if the government were overturned. Once again, Taft headed for Havana. This time, it took twenty, hardworking "awful days" as Taft

45

Tomás Estrada Palma, president of Cuba, asked Taft to return when his government began to fail.

By the time Taft went to Cuba for the second time, he weighed more than 300 pounds (136 kg).

called them, to work out a peaceful solution to the problems.

As soon as Taft came home from Cuba, he was sent to campaign throughout the country. The same *New York Sun* writer who had praised Taft's work suggested that he be called the secretary of peace instead of the secretary of war as he seemed so good at taking care of problems. Taft took all the travel and work right in stride. Although he was a very large man who weighed more than 300 pounds

The Taft Family

★ ★

Nellie and Will's three children, Robert, Charles, and Helen, all grew up to establish substantial careers of their own. Most famous among them was Robert, who served three terms as U.S. senator from Ohio. He earned a reputation as an outstanding conservative senator called "Mr. Republican" for his sweeping influence in party policy-making. His name lives on in the Taft-Hartley Act of 1947, important legislation he co-sponsored that regulates labor-union activity. Robert Taft died in 1953 in the midst of his third term. His brother Charles led a less public life, pursuing a career as a lawyer and serving as mayor of Cincinnati from 1955 to 1957. He died in 1983. Young Helen Taft began her remarkable career as dean of Bryn Mawr College in 1917 at the age of twenty-six. She left in 1920 to marry, earn a Ph.D. in history from Yale, and have two children. Returning to Bryn Mawr in 1925, she served as dean until 1941 and then as a history professor until her retirement in 1957. She also authored two scholarly history books. Helen Taft Manning died in 1987 at the age of ninety-six.

Helen Taft

(136 kg) by that time, he seems to have had a great deal of energy and a quick and intelligent mind. He was good at what he did and liked serving his president and friend, Theodore Roosevelt.

The United States grew during the four years Taft worked in Washington as secretary of war. When Oklahoma became a state in 1907, the number of states rose to 46. The Taft family was also growing up. Helen and Will's daughter, also named Helen, went to her first school dance even though she was a bit shy. After entering the Baldwin School, she grew out of her shyness and even played hockey and basketball. She enjoyed school although she felt her marks were not as good as they should be. She told her parents there was a great deal of work to do there. Her brother Charlie raced around on roller skates and made a lot of noise with his new gramophone and his treasured Kodak camera.

In February 1906, Washington, D.C., enjoyed the grand social event of the wedding of a president's daughter. The much-loved Alice Roosevelt married Nicholas Longworth in a beautiful ceremony in the East Room of the White House. The remaining public rooms were jammed with guests. The Tafts, who had become an important part of the social scene in the capital city, attended the wedding.

During this time, Taft was suffering under the strain of his great weight. He tired easily and often nodded off during public events. Helen poked him with her elbow to wake him when this happened. The strong and determined Helen Taft took control of her husband's diet and exercise and re-

In February 1906, the Tafts attended the wedding of President Roosevelt's daughter Alice.

fused to let him give up. It took nearly six months, but when the spring of 1906 came around, William Howard Taft was down to a physically fit 255 pounds (116 kg). He joked that it was hard work and that the alteration of his clothes cost $400.

Throughout their marriage and his political career, Helen was a help to Will. Her knowledge of music, her organizational skills, her bright mind,

Alice Roosevelt Longworth (1884–1980)

★ ★

No one represented turn-of-the-century America better than the lovely and lively Alice Roosevelt. The oldest daughter of President Theodore Roosevelt, Alice was seventeen when her family moved into the White House. Her outspoken, mischievous manner and her modern good looks won the hearts of Americans. European royalty knew her as the "American Princess," and Kaiser Wilhelm of Germany even named his yacht after her. Women wore dresses of Alice blue, and popular songs traded on her name. The impish Alice came to be known for her flamboyant behavior— smoking, betting, dancing, and drinking whiskey. When critics chided, her exasperated father declared that he could either be president of the United States or he could control Alice, but he could not do both. Her White House wedding to Ohio representative Nicholas Longworth was the social event of 1906. Fond of saying "If you can't say something good about someone, sit right here beside me," Alice later put her scathing wit to good use writing commentary about life in Washington.

This photograph of the Tafts' youngest son, Charlie, was taken in 1906.

and her keen sense of right and wrong were of great help to her husband. Though Helen could have made a name for herself, she chose to make it through her husband. She may have been frustrated that women were so limited, which may be why her sense of humor was not often seen in public.

Several women of Helen Taft's time did make names for themselves without using marriage to do so. Contemporaries of Helen included Jane Addams, who never married but spent her energies on her work with immigrants. Another woman of the time

Robert A. Taft, Helen and Will's firstborn son, as a student at Yale

Chicago social worker Jane Addams was a contemporary of Helen Taft's.

The day nursery at Hull House, a social settlement house in Chicago opened by Jane Addams

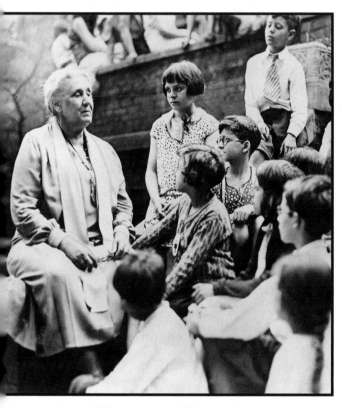

Jane Addams is pictured here with a group of immigrant children.

period was Charlotte Perkins Gilman, who shocked people by divorcing her husband and giving him custody of their daughter. Charlotte then embarked on her own career as a speaker and writer.

Since Helen chose to find her fame and power through her husband, her roles often changed as he took new positions. As wife of the governor of the Philippines, she lived in luxury for three years. When Will became secretary of war, Helen had a new set of challenges as she took on the role of a cabinet wife in Washington, D.C. She

The Taft family about 1906: Standing left to right behind Nellie are Will, Helen, Charlie, and Robert.

was expected to call on or visit the wives of other cabinet members and to receive them one day a week at her home. The women spent much time gossiping, and Helen had to pretend to be interested. She herself found this visiting to be a rather "monotonous stress." She also didn't enjoy being one of the cabinet wives instead of the First Lady as she had been in the Philippines.

As usual, Helen did what was right and patiently spent her time speaking up to help her husband's career. She often became so interested in a Senate debate that she would miss lunch. She could debate politics with most men and spent much time going over Taft's speeches and giving him confidence to continue in his work. However much she might have wished that she could be a politician, the role of political partner to Will was her main concern. Will also helped his own career because he was a man people trusted and looked up to. He was very intelligent and had his own opinions about most issues. He was never afraid to voice these opinions or to act on his values.

One such opinion was that innocent people should not be discriminated against because of their skin color. Will had learned to help people from his father's example. He often expressed concern with the way African Americans were being treated in the United States. He declared that he had no race prejudice but knowing that such feelings existed made him sorry for those whose lives were hurt by hate. Helen was also known as a woman free of racism. This was seen in the way she dealt with the people of the Philippines and how thrilling she found her adventures in Hawaii.

Helen Taft also supported a woman's right to get an education and have her own career outside of marriage. She supported women by writing letters for those who wanted a government job. She believed women should be allowed to discuss all topics including politics and even believed they should be able to vote. Helen did not believe that women should be elected or appointed to government office but had no problem with women helping their husbands get elected or appointed.

African Americans in the Twentieth Century's First Decade

✹ ✹ ✹ ✹ ✹ ✹ ✹ ✹ ✹ ✹ ✹ ✹ ✹ ✹ ✹ ✹ ✹ ✹ ✹ ✹

The Tafts might well have been disturbed at the plight of America's black people around the turn of the twentieth century. Forty years after the Civil War, African Americans were still struggling for equality. Even though the Civil Rights Act of 1875 guaranteed them certain rights, racism and prejudice grew stronger. To make matters worse, the Supreme Court handed down several decisions that limited protection for black people and diminished penalties for discrimination. In 1896, the court ruled that it was legal to offer "separate but equal" services to blacks and whites. This historic case opened the floodgates to legalized segregation—the enforced separation of one group from another. A deluge of "Jim Crow" laws—which segregated schools, restaurants, and public transportation into strictly separate black and white sections—were passed, especially in the South. Georgia established separate parks; Oklahoma mandated separate phone booths. Drinking fountains, restrooms, and elevators were restricted to one race or the other. The humiliation of enforced segregation became a way of life for African Americans in the first decade of the twentieth century and lasted sixty years. Finally, when the Supreme Court ruled against segregated schools in 1954, the Jim Crow laws began to topple and a new era of civil-rights activism began.

William Howard Taft had turned down his first chance to be appointed a justice to the Supreme Court in 1902 because he wanted to finish his work in the Philippines. In 1908, when Roosevelt's second presidential term was ending, he made it clear that he wanted Taft to run for president. Taft thought of saying no and waiting for a chance to be appointed to the Supreme Court, his lifelong dream. Helen Taft and Will's brothers talked him into changing his mind. Helen once admitted that her greatest fear was that Will would say no to the presidency.

Taft, who had a great deal of experience in both foreign policy and

affairs at home, was thought to be an excellent choice for president. He won the nomination of the Republican Party and James S. Sherman, a congressman from New York, was nominated as his running mate. Taft's Democratic Party opponent was William Jennings Bryan, who had run

Taft receiving the news from President Roosevelt that he had been nominated for president

This 1908 Republican presidential campaign banner, headlined "The Nations Choice," shows pictures of William Howard Taft and his running mate, James S. Sherman.

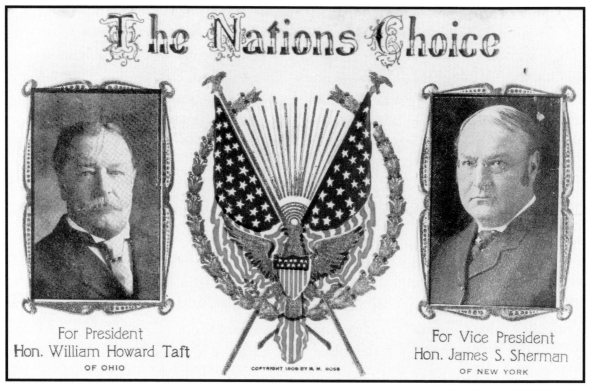

The Nations Choice

For President
Hon. William Howard Taft
OF OHIO

COPYRIGHT 1908 BY M. M. ROSS

For Vice President
Hon. James S. Sherman
OF NEW YORK

twice before for the office of president. Taft won the election by a large number of votes. On March 4, 1909, just three months before her forty-eighth birthday, Helen Taft's dream had come true. She was about to move into the White House for a four-year tenure as the First Lady of the land.

A commemorative tin plate in honor of the Republican nominees in the 1908 presidential election

Republican presidential nominee William Howard Taft giving an impassioned speech during the 1908 campaign, which led to his election as president of the United States

Taft's Democratic presidential opponent, William Jennings Bryan

CHAPTER FOUR

The White House Years

★ ★ ★ ★ ★ ★ ★ ★ ★ ★ ★ ★ ★ ★ ★ ★

In her autobiography, Helen Taft mentions that both she and President Roosevelt thought that Will was not a very eager campaigner. Roosevelt was so concerned about Taft and his lack of excitement over running for president that Teddy told Will he might not back him for the nomination.

This terrified Helen. She had spent most of her adult life getting Will to this place, the presidential nomination, and now he might damage his chances. There was no way Helen was going to let that happen. As an intelligent and determined woman, she might have made a better candidate than her husband. Will

★ ★ ★ ★ ★ ★ ★ ★ ★ ★ ★ ★ ★ ★ ★ ★

The Taft family in their chauffeured 1908 Stanley Steamer

President Theodore Roosevelt (left) with Taft just before Taft's inauguration as president

himself admitted that the presidency was not the prize he had hoped to capture. His dream was the Supreme Court.

Will wrote to Roosevelt saying that he would understand if Roosevelt had to back another man and there would not be any hard feelings on his part. Roosevelt replied that Mrs. Taft had misunderstood him. He only wanted Will to show his interest and make sure his supporters would not lose heart. William Howard Taft had never turned his back on public duty or his wife's advice, so when Helen told him he needed to be more interested and

Helen Taft was the first First Lady to ride in the Inaugural Parade in the presidential carriage

President Taft (center) reviewing the inaugural festivities

excited and to make sure that President Roosevelt knew he wanted to run for the office, he did it.

Regardless of whether or not William Howard Taft thought he would be a good president, Roosevelt pushed for him and the people supported him. He was elected for one four-year term that began in 1909 and ended in 1913.

On his inauguration day, Washington, D.C., was hit by a terrible blizzard. Taft joked that even nature didn't want him in the White House. When the snow finally stopped, the festivities went on. Helen Taft was the first of the First Ladies to break tradition and ride in the same carriage with her husband as it rolled along in the parade. Until then, wives followed in a second or third carriage. Helen, however, had fought too hard to get here and refused to be anywhere but in the main carriage with Will. She even admitted to a secret delight in doing something that no other woman had ever done. From that time on, First Ladies rode with their husbands.

As president, Taft is known for many important accomplishments

The United States and Its Territories

☆ ☆

Since the American Revolution, the United States has expanded more than four times in size. To grow beyond the thirteen original states located on the eastern seaboard, Congress carved out territories to explore and settle. In these regions, territorial governments were established, but they had no say in Washington. That would come with statehood. Congress established the first territory in 1787 on land northwest of the Ohio River. Gradually, all the land in the Northwest Territory became the states around the Great Lakes. Americans organized other territories as they pushed farther west. Each territory became a state when enough

President Taft signing the proclamation that made Arizona the forty-eighth state

people lived there and an acceptable government had been established. Finally, during Will Taft's presidency, New Mexico and Arizona—territories since the mid-1800s—were admitted to the Union as the forty-seventh and forty-eighth states. By then, U.S. territorial claims extended beyond its boundaries to include possessions in the Pacific and Caribbean. But, as William Taft discovered in the Philippines, governing distant lands was made difficult by issues of race and culture. Of those remote territories, only Alaska and Hawaii became states. The Philippine Islands gained full independence on July 4, 1946. Today, the main U.S. territories are the Virgin Islands, Guam, and American Samoa. The self-governing Commonwealth of Puerto Rico is closest to becoming a state, though the idea is controversial among Puerto Ricans.

that were good for the nation. Both New Mexico and Arizona joined the Union to make a total of 48 states, and the population of the country grew to more than 97 million. The first junior high school was opened in Ohio. Taft appointed six new judges to the Supreme Court. He is credited with the establishment of the Post Office Department in 1910 and adding the Department of Labor to the president's cabinet. During Taft's term, the Sixteenth Amendment to the Constitution was passed, giving Congress the right to collect income taxes.

Taft, who loved sports, threw out the first baseball to open the 1910 baseball season in the game between the Washington Senators and the Philadelphia Athletics. This became a presidential tradition, and to this day, baseball seasons begin each year with this custom. Taft also tried to create a balanced federal budget by asking each department to turn in accounts of their financial needs. During his term as president, Alaska received full territorial government, a step toward becoming a state. The United States made loans to countries needing

President Taft threw out the first ball to open the 1910 Washington Senators' baseball season.

money. This was called "dollar diplomacy," as it helped Taft increase the influence of America on governments that owed money to the United States. Taft also pushed a bill through Congress that required politicians to make their campaign funding public information. He was part of the committee that finally got the Lincoln Memorial completed and chose the site in Potomac Park where it stands today. Taft was a busy president and had little time to think about the Supreme Court. He often remembered his mother saying "uneasy lies the

A 1909 photograph of the First Family (left to right), Helen, Will, Nellie, Charlie, and Robert

Helen's pet project was to bring Japan's beautiful cherry trees to the capital. The mayor of Tokyo contributed 3,000 trees, which were planted around the Tidal Basin and still draw thousands of visitors to Washington every spring.

head that wears a crown." This was a figure of speech, of course, since Taft did not actually wear a crown, though he held the highest political office in the country.

While President Taft was busy, so was his wife Helen. Some people think she was so busy that her frantic pace led to her becoming ill and having a stroke only two months after her husband took office. No one knows exactly what caused the stroke, but it did leave her without speech and slightly paralyzed. Before she became ill, Mrs. Taft was a skillful hostess and enjoyed her role as First Lady at White House functions. She also enjoyed entertaining friends at small tea parties in the White House. As soon as the Tafts moved into the White House, Helen replaced the male steward with a female housekeeper and fired many doormen, cooks, and other staff members so that she could give jobs to people of color.

As a result of her visits to Japan on the way to and from the Philippines, Helen was able to bring something of great beauty and importance to Washington. She had been enchanted with the Japanese cherry blossom festival and wanted the American people to have a similar tradition. She also thought it would be nice for tourists to see a beautified city, especially since Potomac Park was a swampy, mosquito-infested part of the city. Helen asked all the nurseries in America to send their cherry trees to Washington. She was disappointed when only 100 arrived, but the mayor of Tokyo sent her between 2,000 and 3,000 cherry trees for her project as a gift to the American people. Unfortunately, the first batch of trees arrived infected with disease and had to be destroyed. The mayor sent a second batch of 3,000 trees that were just fine. These beautiful spring-blooming cherry trees were planted around the Tidal Basin and still draw thousands of visitors to the capital city every spring. Not until nearly fifty years later, with the work of Lady Bird Johnson, did a First Lady take so much interest in beautifying the city. This is Helen Taft's lasting legacy to the American people and all those who visit from foreign lands.

When Helen Taft suffered her stroke in 1909, it was a frightening ex-

These two photographs of the elegant First Lady Helen Herron Taft were taken after she suffered a stroke only two months after Will took office as president.

perience for the whole family. She had been hostess at several dinners, luncheons, and teas and had actually entertained all the important members of the House of Representatives and all the senators and their wives in less than two months. On the day of her stroke, her son Charlie had his adenoids removed, which had distressed her. The Tafts were sailing down the Potomac River to Mount Vernon, the historical home of George Washington, when she became ill. People thought she had just fainted, but to be safe, the yacht was turned around. Mrs. Taft was only half-conscious when she was taken to her room in the White House. She slept for sixteen hours, and the doctor said she would recover. Then they realized she had suffered a massive stroke. Her collapse was kept secret from the public for several weeks. The newspapers reported that she was ill but said nothing of the stroke. Her sisters took turns visiting her and helped out by fulfilling her hostess duties. The flowers from the White House greenhouses cheered her. She had them put throughout the White House private areas and public rooms, and even sent carnations to Will's office.

President Taft trusted and relied on his wife's political good sense. She may have been able to control the Republican Party better than Taft did if she hadn't been ill. It took Helen over a year to recover. Even then, her doctors were surprised that she recovered at all. But we know how determined a person she was. Helen worked day and night to regain her speech, tighten her drooping facial muscles, and regain the use of her arms. Taft took time out of every day to read to her and help her learn to speak again. Her daughter, Helen, was also a big help. She left college for a year to take over her mother's hostess duties during this time.

Helen eventually regained her speech, although she never again made long speeches and kept her speaking engagements to a minimum. The family's love and concern for Helen could be seen in everything they did for her as she learned how to dress herself and comb her hair, to write, and to use her limbs again. The American people did not know what had happened to the First Lady and many thought she had taken ill and withdrawn from society. Not Helen!

On the Tafts' silver wedding anniversary, June 19, 1911, a glorious party was given at the White House. The decorations and food were wonderful. Multicolored lights outlined the White House, and all the trees and bushes on the grounds were decorated with lights. Spotlights shone on the American flag that waved above the White House. More than 3,000 guests attended the party. Helen

The First Family (left to right), Charlie, Nellie, Helen, Will, and Robert, posed for this photograph on the occasion of Nellie and Will's twenty-fifth wedding anniversary.

looked like a queen in a beautiful white gown. But she wasn't totally well yet. Her daughter greeted people around the room, as she herself could not do much moving and walking. Helen sat at her table to receive the guests who wished her well on her recovery and on the occasion of her twenty-fifth wedding anniversary.

Because she was ill and spending so much time and effort to recover, Helen was not, at this time, very involved in the women's fight for the vote. If she had been well, perhaps Helen would have pushed Taft to promote the vote for women during his presidency. But this did not happen. Most First Ladies take on a cause or work for an organization that is trying to make a contribution to the country.

The view from the South Portico of the White House was Helen's favorite, and she was often photographed sitting there.

Helen didn't have much chance to do this. She didn't fully recover until Taft's term was nearly over. Even then, she still had speech problems and physical pain. Standing for long periods of time was difficult, and so Helen decided to do away with tradition and sit or wear flat shoes. Her family knew how hard it was for her and how bitterly disappointed she was to miss so much of her time as First Lady, espe-

cially after dreaming of it for so many years. The sadness his wife's condition caused him may have contributed to Will's unhappiness as president.

The Tafts spent many peaceful hours sitting on the South Portico of the White House listening to favorite phonograph recordings. The view from the South Portico was Helen's favorite, and she was often photographed there. Taft spent his free time playing golf and tennis and horseback riding. For a large man, he was graceful and athletic. Taft even enjoyed dancing. Many evenings at the White House were planned as musicales, and Mrs. Taft invited many talented artists, musicians, and writers to entertain the First Family and their many guests. She liked all types of art, and one of her garden parties featured a group of Sioux dancers.

Helen made other changes at the White House. Cars took the place of horse-drawn carriages, and White House meals were prepared by the staff. Previously, all meals had been brought in from restaurants. Helen was shocked to discover that the president was expected to pay for meals at

During Taft's presidency, he spent his free time playing golf (above) and tennis and horse riding.

ever he had gained too much weight, he would be served a steak of only 8 ounces (227 g)! To accommodate their many guests, Helen Taft made use of the china that had been purchased by many First Ladies before her. Today, visitors to the White House can see the many china patterns on display in the China Room. One of these sets of china was commissioned by First Lady Lucy Hayes. These beautiful dishes and serving pieces, with pictures of American wildlife and plants, were hand painted by an American artist. Mrs. Hayes wanted to preserve American wildlife as it looked in her day for futhre Americans.

Toward the end of Taft's term in office, it became clear that former President Theodore Roosevelt was going to run for the office again, on the Progressive Party ticket. Even Helen Taft was weary. All the entertaining and her long and difficult recovery from her stroke had weakened her. She still felt quite ill at times. Taft, who had not wanted to be president in the first place, was just about ready to leave. The Republicans, however, talked him into running again. Both Taft and

a cost of $7.50 per person. She put a stop to this and, from that time on, presidents have had their own cooks at the White House.

As president, Taft often invited dinner guests at the last minute—often large numbers of them. Helen had to be ready to entertain at any time. Taft often invited people for breakfast, which for him included two oranges, toast and jelly, a 12-ounce (340-gram) steak, and coffee. When-

The End of a Friendship

★ ★ ★ ★ ★ ★ ★ ★ ★ ★ ★ ★ ★ ★ ★ ★ ★ ★ ★ ★

Though they were both large and active men, no two friends could have been more different than the outgoing Teddy Roosevelt and the thoughtful Will Taft. Yet friends they were, since the days Taft had served President Roosevelt so well as secretary of war and close adviser. Though Roosevelt really wanted to run for a second term in 1908, he kept his promise that he wouldn't. He concentrated his legendary energy on the nomination and election of Will Taft, "the most lovable personality I have ever come in contact with." Taft, however, proved a reluctant candidate, nervous about filling TR's shoes. His instincts turned out to be correct. Though he tried to "complete and perfect" Roosevelt's goals, the honest and earnest President Taft couldn't hold the conservative and progressive factions of the Republican Party together. Disappointed and angered by Taft's presidency, TR rose to run against him in 1912 as the leader of a new party called the Progressives. TR called his one-time friend "useless to the American people," a puzzlewit, and a fathead. Taft responded less theatrically. In a three-way race, both men lost to Democrat Woodrow Wilson. Saddened by their fading friendship, Taft wrote that it was "very hard to see a devoted friendship going to pieces like a rope of sand."

Roosevelt were defeated by Woodrow Wilson. With fewer regrets than one might imagine, the Tafts left the White House in 1913.

A cartoon published during the 1912 presidential campaign

69

CHAPTER FIVE

Women and Their Roles during Helen's Time

★ ★ ★ ★ ★ ★ ★ ★ ★ ★ ★ ★ ★ ★ ★ ★

Helen was politically ambitious, and enhancing her husband's image was her prime goal. She was the first president's wife to lend her gown to the new First Ladies Collection at the National Museum of American History at the Smithsonian Institution in Washington, D.C. Anyone visiting the museum would see her gown and think of her husband.

Two special tools that a politician's wife used to further her husband's career were the "calling card" and the "at-home card." Like business cards of today, but slightly larger and very elegantly printed on fine paper,

★ ★ ★ ★ ★ ★ ★ ★ ★ ★ ★ ★ ★ ★ ★ ★

One of First Lady
Helen Herron Taft's
"at-home" cards

Mrs. Taft
At Home
Friday afternoon
May fourteenth
from five until seven o'clock

One of First Lady Helen Herron Taft's "at-home" cards

these cards were part of the custom of paying official calls to politically important Washington wives. A woman visited other women on their at-home days and left her calling card to announce that she had been there. She also left her at-home card so women would know what day she expected to be visited in return. The wives would then tell their husbands who had come to call that day and what they had discussed. In this way, women were able to get their husband's ideas, names, and reputations known to the community. Helen Taft was very good at helping Will to gain political friends and backers.

Another custom of Helen's day was to print a prominent woman's signature or photograph on handkerchiefs to give to other women as souvenirs. During the holidays of Christmas and Easter, Helen also autographed pictures of the White House showing the South Portico. She sent these autographed pictures to women who asked for souvenirs. Mrs. Taft recalls that she never refused these requests and must

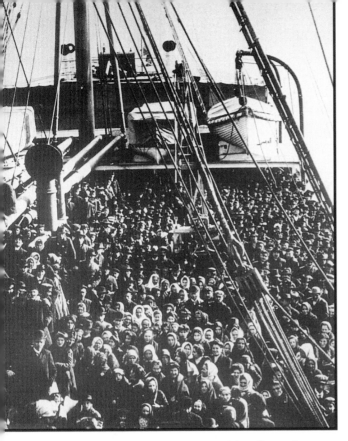

These immigrants were among 14 million who arrived in the United States between 1900 and 1910.

Frances Benjamin Johnston (above) photographed many First Ladies, including Helen Taft.

have sent many because they were ordered by the hundreds.

America grew rapidly in the years between 1900 and 1920. In fact, 14 million new immigrants came to the United States. These new people brought their foods, their styles of dress, and other examples of their cultural backgrounds with them. Soon, Americans everywhere were using foreign phrases and enjoying previously unfamiliar foods.

During the time Helen and Will were in the White House, women accomplished many "firsts." In 1909, Frances Benjamin Johnston, a photographer of important men and women in Washington, D.C., photographed First Lady Helen Taft. She had photographed every First Lady from Carolyn Harrison to Helen Taft, often

73

This woman suffrage march, one of many that supported the right of women to vote, took place on May 20, 1911.

showing the First Ladies in serious poses at their desks or in less formal poses with their children.

The following year, in 1910, women in their college academic robes marched down New York City's Fifth Avenue to promote women's right to vote. Also in 1910, Mabel

Bacon became the first woman to take part in a power-boat race and won second place at the Kennebec Yacht Club in Maine. In 1911, the first women's agricultural training school was opened in Long Island, New York, with twenty students. More than 625 women had applied the first year. Margaret Sanger, a nurse, began devoting herself to the cause of birth control in 1912. In 1913, the last year of William Howard Taft's term as president, Georgia Broadwick became the first woman to parachute from an airplane.

At about the time Helen Taft was moving into the White House, women were also developing into good athletes. Basketball, under the leadership of Sendra Berenson at Smith College, had already become a favorite sport of college women. During the Taft presidency, high-school girls were beginning to play basketball. It was very much a girls' game at this time. Boys rarely, if ever, played basketball because it was considered too "female"! By the early 1900s, baseball, field hockey, golf, swimming, and "balls and rackets"—or tennis as Americans called the game—were

In 1913, the last year of President Taft's term in office, Georgia Broadwick became the first woman to parachute from an airplane.

Sendra Berenson of Smith College helped make basketball a favorite sport of college women.

Members of a 1912 suburban Philadelphia "feminine" baseball club

A girls' high-school basketball team plays a game in Brookline, Massachusetts.

By the early 1900s, golf (above), baseball, field hockey, swimming, and "balls and rackets"—or tennis—(below) were extremely popular with women athletes.

In 1869, Wyoming became the first state to give women the right to vote.

also extremely popular with women athletes.

Women athletes were not allowed to compete in the first modern Olympic Games in 1896. However, the 1900 games featured women's golf and tennis. By 1908, women were allowed to compete in archery and figure skating. As new timesaving inventions appeared in America, women had more time to be athletically involved in these new barrier-

Winning the Right to Vote

☆ ☆ ☆ ☆ ☆ ☆ ☆ ☆ ☆ ☆ ☆ ☆ ☆ ☆ ☆ ☆ ☆ ☆ ☆ ☆

As a conservative, President Taft did not support woman suffrage—the right of women to vote. By the time he took office, however, women's struggle to participate in national elections had reached a fever pitch and there would be no stopping it. The struggle had begun in 1848 at the first women's-rights convention, held in Seneca Falls, New York. The women there drew up a manifesto called the "Declaration of Sentiments." It called for equality for women, including the right to vote. Every year since 1878, a woman suffrage amendment was introduced in Congress. Every year it failed to pass. Indeed, though many states allowed their female residents to vote in certain elections, national law continued to reserve that right for men. Many people agreed with Taft, believing that women were not smart enough to cast a ballot intelligently. Couldn't men represent their wives best? And what would happen to family life if women won the right to vote?

By the Tafts' day, however, as more women went to college and took jobs, their voices grew louder in support of woman suffrage and other social reforms such as child labor laws, civil rights for African Americans, prison reform, and an end to political corruption. They won their battle for the vote in 1919, when Congress finally passed the Nineteenth Amendment. It became law in 1920, and promised that "The right of citizens of the United States to vote shall not be denied or abridged on account of sex."

breaking individual or team sports. Some women, however, used their free time to break different barriers.

In 1869, Wyoming gave women the vote as an incentive for women settlers to come to the far-off area. Slowly, over the next thirty-five years, most of the western states gave women some, if not all, voting rights. In the rest of the United States, however, lawmakers believed that women were not able to think clearly enough to vote intelligently. Helen rarely mentioned women's voting rights in her autobiography. It is a bit of a mystery that suffrage was not a major concern in her life, since we know that she was ambitious, politically aware, and very intelligent.

There are several possible reasons why Helen Taft did not become an active fighter for women's rights. When the movement for suffrage was gaining momentum in the first years of the twentieth century, the Tafts were in the Philippines. The cause of women's voting rights would have been far from the mind of a woman interested in furthering her husband's career. By the time Will was running for president, Helen may have thought she should behave like the typical political wife who kept her opinions to herself so as not to cost her husband votes. Also, after moving into the White House, Helen had only a few months as First Lady before being incapacitated by a stroke.

Even though Helen did not participate in the fight for women's rights, the suffrage movement was a large part of the lives of many women in her time. Huge numbers of women with both Caucasian and African-American backgrounds worked for years to convince other women and men that women were able to make sensible voting decisions.

Mary Coffin Ware Dennett, the national suffrage corresponding secretary, sent out millions of pamphlets throughout the country during the years between 1910 and 1914. She was also a pioneer in the movement for birth control and sex education.

A founder of the Women's Peace Party and a believer that women

Mary Coffin Ware Dennett was the national suffrage corresponding secretary.

Charlotte Anna Perkins Stetson Gilman was a founder of the Women's Peace Party and wrote at length about women's rights.

should have their own money, Charlotte Anna Perkins Stetson Gilman wrote many magazine articles and books about women's rights. Iowan Jessie Annette Jack Hooper established a kindergarten, a visiting nurses program, and a tuberculosis hospital.

Addie D. Waites Hunton, who worked with black troops during World War I, is known for her statement that "No women are free until all women are free." Daisy Adams Lampkin was a civil-rights reformer, community leader, and promoter of

woman suffrage among black women in Pittsburgh, Pennsylvania. She was also an active organizer of the National Association for the Advancement of Colored People (NAACP). The first African-American woman to become a trained nurse, Mary Elizabeth Mahoney was a strong supporter of women's rights and one of the first women to register to vote.

Ida B. Wells, also known as Ida Wells-Barnett, who lost her parents to yellow fever when she was only fourteen years old, refused to give up her

Ida B. Wells led campaigns against lynching and marched in suffrage parades.

Florence Kelley was a Quaker who fought for a minimum wage and an end to child labor.

railroad seat to move to the "colored section." She then sued the railroad. Wells wrote articles, led national campaigns against lynching (hanging of blacks without a trial), and protested the exclusion of black people from the World's Columbian Exposition. She also marched in Washington, D.C., parades for suffrage. Mary Eliza Church Terrell, whose mother was a former slave and whose father was the first African-American millionaire in the South, was a Washington, D.C., community leader who picketed the White House for suffrage.

Florence Kelley, a Quaker who fought for a minimum wage and an end to child labor, led the National Consumer's League in New York City. She led reforms in factories and city slums, and still managed to attend evening law school. Alice Stokes Paul, also a

Quaker, was the chief strategy person for the militant wing of the suffrage movement. She organized parades and hunger strikes to get her point across and was jailed three times.

Active in Wisconsin, Belle Case LaFollette was the wife of Senator Robert M. LaFollette Sr. She worked and wrote for peace and racial equality. Mary Park Woods, the organizer of the College Equal Suffrage League, was active in Washington, D.C., Boston, and Maine.

Jeannette Pickering Rankin lobbied in fifteen states for woman suffrage. The first woman elected to Congress, she voted against both World Wars. Anna Howard Shaw, the first ordained female Methodist minister, was an outstanding suffrage speaker who spoke in every state in the country.

While writing an anti-suffrage article, Harriet Taylor Upton became a suffrage convert. She wrote articles that pointed out the importance and work of women in building up the nation.

Belle Case LaFollette worked and wrote for peace and racial equality.

Jeannette Rankin, who lobbied for woman suffrage, was the first woman elected to Congress.

Among the most well-known woman suffrage leaders were Susan B. Anthony (above left), Elizabeth Cady Stanton (above right), Lucretia Mott (below left), and Sojourner Truth (below right).

The year William Howard Taft took office, Lila Hardaway Meade Valentine was chosen head of the Equal Suffrage League of Virginia. Later, she made speeches throughout Virginia to support women's rights.

During the years Taft was president, Maud Younger, a millionaire, worked as a waitress and lived in a poor section of town to learn what it was like. She helped win the eight-hour-day labor law for California and spoke all over the state for the suffrage movement.

Other suffrage leaders such as Susan B. Anthony, Lucretia Mott, Elizabeth Cady Stanton, Carrie Chapman Catt, Sojourner Truth, and Lucy Stone and her daughter Alice Stone Blackwell are more well known. However, each of these women, famous or not, played an important role and helped to fight for the women's movement. All of them made huge contributions to the cause of voting rights and civil rights at a time when at least 50 percent of the population thought women were meant only to have children and raise them. The women's movement might have been mainly about voting rights and working rights, but it also pointed out the need for democracy to be extended to a class of people who had been left out since the Constitution was written. By working together, women across the country accomplished their goals, and the Nineteenth Amendment to the Constitution, which gave women the right to vote, was finally ratified in 1920.

Helen Taft's accomplishments during her time as First Lady may seem small compared to those of other women who had one or two full terms in the White House. However, in the brief time she was healthy, Helen gave the city of Washington, D.C., two wonderful gifts. Because Helen had loved music all her life, she arranged for a bandstand to be built in Potomac Park. Music lovers attended the Marine Band Concerts held there. Anyone who has visited Washington or seen pictures of the city in the spring cannot help but notice the beautiful cherry blossom trees that line the Tidal Basin. Each year, these blooms make Washington look like a fairy-tale city, thanks to Helen Herron Taft.

CHAPTER SIX

More to Come after the Presidency

✶ ✶ ✶ ✶ ✶ ✶ ✶ ✶ ✶ ✶ ✶ ✶ ✶ ✶ ✶ ✶

William Howard Taft was glad to retire from politics to serve as Kent Professor of Law at Yale University. Helen Taft, who had spent much of her married life helping her husband become president, began to live a much different life after the Tafts left the White House. The move from president to professor was not hard for either Will or Helen. When the couple arrived at Yale on an April day in 1913, they were welcomed by a great number of students who cheered and sang. Will said just being on the campus made him feel young again.

✶ ✶ ✶ ✶ ✶ ✶ ✶ ✶ ✶ ✶ ✶ ✶ ✶ ✶ ✶ ✶

When Chief Justice Edward D. White died in 1921, President Warren G. Harding appointed Taft to the position, the one he had always wanted. Chief Justice Taft (front, center) is shown here with his Court.

In Taft's time, professors wore black robes. His were tailored to fit him, which helped hide his huge size. Students enjoyed seeing him on the campus and were impressed to find him in the library doing his own research for classes. He was a gentle and good teacher and much loved by the students. After having been so badly beaten by Woodrow Wilson in the presidential election, this university position was good for both Will and Helen.

Helen settled into a quieter and simpler routine of daily life than she had known in the White House. Guests to their home were surprised that the front door was answered by the former First Lady herself! Her days were spent in relaxing pastimes such as golf, concerts, and the theater. While Helen entertained and made new friends, Taft was busy being the best professor he could be. His students were impressed by his work habits and cheered his lectures. They thought it was amazing to have a former president for a professor. The second month that the Tafts were at Yale, Helen had problems with bleeding in one eye, but much to William's peace of mind, it was not another stroke.

When the chief justice of the Supreme Court, Edward D. White, died in 1921, William Howard Taft was named to the office, the one he

The Other Supremes

✯ ✯

The Supreme Court, on which the young Will Taft set his sights, is the highest court in the United States. As chief justice, Taft assumed the role of the nation's top judge, overseeing the work of the eight associate justices. Since its first session in 1790, the Court has protected and interpreted the U.S. Constitution, which outlines the supreme law of the land. To do so, the Court reviews cases that are appealed to it from lower courts. The Supreme Court receives around 5,000 appeals each year, but hears only about 180 during its session between October and April. In May and June, the Court delivers opinions reached over the term. By this process, the Court decides whether certain federal and state laws contradict the spirit and intent of the U.S. Constitution and should therefore be overridden. Its landmark decisions dealing with slavery, civil rights, and abortion have shaped American history. Chief Justice Taft himself helped to streamline this process by working to pass the Judiciary Act in 1925, which gave the Court more power to select cases of national importance to review. Taft left the Court another legacy when he convinced Congress to construct a building to house the Supreme Court, which had been meeting in the Capitol for most of its life. Sadly, he didn't live to see the Court's new home, completed in 1935.

Taft became the first person in American history to be both a president and a chief justice.

Chief Justice William Howard Taft with his wife, Helen Herron Taft

The Tafts vacationed in this house in Murray Bay, Quebec, Canada.

had always truly wanted. President Warren G. Harding appointed Taft to the position, making Will the first person in America's history to be both a president and a chief justice.

Although Helen's health was not very good, she went to Washington with her husband when he took up his new position. Taft brought harmony and efficiency to the Supreme Court.

Helen was once again a Washington wife, but her health kept her from doing a great deal of socializing.

People still loved her, however, and she was never completely out of the public eye. She continued to be Will's closest adviser and partner.

Will and Helen made a trip to England in 1922. The visit was a high point of Will's life, as he enjoyed being a widely well-known public person. Helen delighted in meeting the prime minister and other important people. Will was amused when the Prince of Wales (son of the Queen of England) remarked that Will had done well after the presidency and that "hadn't he been put in the cabinet, or something?"

This photograph of Will and Helen vacationing in Murray Bay with their children and grandchildren was taken during the time Will was chief justice.

The caisson carrying William Howard Taft's flag-draped casket is shown here as it passed the White House on the way to the Capitol.

Unfortunately, Will's hard work and long hours began to take a toll on him. He had two heart attacks, was required to spend some time in bed, and had to take heart medicines. It seemed as if his energy was sapped and his strength was gone. In 1930, Taft was forced to resign his position as chief justice of the Supreme Court because of his failing health.

Will and Helen spent their evenings reading and sitting together talking of the early days in Cincinnati.

Helen installed an elevator in their brick house and made other changes so that everyday life would be easier for Will. He was not able to make use of the improvements, however, as he died only one month after his retirement. This seventy-two-year-old man who had so lovingly cared for and watched over his wife's heart and health, died in Washington, D.C., on March 3, 1930. Helen was only sixty-nine years old, and grieved greatly for him. Because she did not want to go

A National Resting Place

★ ★

The Tafts share their final resting place at Arlington National Cemetery with more than 200,000 other souls. Occupying 612 acres (248 hectares) of rolling hillside overlooking the Potomac River just outside of Washington, D.C., this vast national shrine was established as a Civil War burial ground. Today, American soldiers from every war since the Revolution rest at Arlington, along with thousands of other military personnel. Heavyweight boxer Joe Louis and detective novelist Dashiell Hammett, both soldiers during World War II, are buried here as are America's youngest soldier and the first woman army surgeon. Two U.S. presidents, John F. Kennedy and Taft, rest at Arlington. The Tomb of the Unknowns contains the remains of one unidentified soldier from World Wars I and II and the Korean War. These three soldiers, forever nameless, silently represent all of America's war dead. Since the remains of James Blassie, once the unknown Vietnam serviceman, were identified and returned to his family in 1998, no one has taken his place in the tomb.

back to Ohio, the place she had tried so hard to escape as a young married woman, she remained in Washington until her own death many years later. Helen lived alone in the house she and Will had shared.

Ever interested in politics and the women behind the men elected to of-

After Will died, Nellie was as active as possible and founded the Anna Louise Inn for poor girls (left).

fice, Helen became a friend of First Lady Grace Coolidge and continued to be as socially active as her health allowed. She especially enjoyed attending concerts of the music she loved and traveling as often as possible. Helen also established the Anna Louise Inn for poor girls and became one of the honorary vice presidents of the Girl Scouts.

Preferring a geology lecture to a luncheon, Helen was often thought of as a woman who had a mind of her own and did as she pleased. She was determined to be heard in a time when it was not very fashionable for women to enter business or a profession. Helen and Will had been partners throughout their marriage, and he relied on her for advice and guid-

The Taft monument in Arlington National Cemetery, where both Will and Helen are buried

Helen is shown here as she left the White House after meeting with President Franklin Roosevelt in 1938.

92

Charles P. Taft, the Tafts' youngest son, became mayor of Cincinnati.

Robert A. Taft, the family's firstborn son, became a powerful and respected senator from Ohio.

Helen Taft Manning, the Tafts' only daughter, was dean of Bryn Mawr College for a time.

ance. This is rare in the White House, as First Ladies are not encouraged to become too involved in the work of the presidency.

Helen was a woman of strength and courage, but suffered from exhaustion and ill health. She tended to throw herself into every project, often doing too much at one time. Helen skrimped on costs wherever she could, and by the time the Tafts left the White House, she had saved many hundreds of thousands of dollars.

Never able to sit back and let the world go by, Helen continued to push herself and to get the most out of her life. She traveled around the world more than once, and although as a woman she had enjoyed political power and prestige through her husband and as his adviser, she refused to speak out publicly for woman suffrage or to advance the rights of women.

Helen Taft lived through the Great Depression, a period of great economic trouble in America. She also kept up with politics in Washington and befriended other First Ladies. She spent time with her children and was very proud of all of their accomplishments. Her daughter had great leanings toward women's rights, and it seems that Helen never tried to convince her to change. Helen continued to be her own person until her death in 1943, thirteen years after Will's death.

Former President and Chief Justice William Howard Taft was the first president to be buried at Arlington National Cemetery. This is a special cemetery where war heroes and veterans are buried. It was a great honor to be the first president buried there. His grave is marked by a tall granite monument. When Helen Herron Taft died, she became the first of all the First Ladies to be buried with her husband in the national cemetery.

Portrait of America, 1943: From War to War

✯ ✯

Born at the start of the Civil War, Helen Herron Taft died eighty-two years later as the United States entered its second year in World War II. It was a grim business, as the Allied forces struggled to stem the power of Nazi Germany, Japan, and Italy. About 60,000 Americans had already perished. By the end of 1943, however, Allied victories in North Africa, Italy, and the Pacific had turned the tide, and plans were well underway for the ultimate invasion of Europe on June 6, 1944, which became known as D-Day.

Back home, under the leadership of President Franklin D. Roosevelt, the nation trembled and cheered as more than 16 million young Americans marched off to fight. Those not fighting threw themselves into the war effort in other ways. Faced with food rationing, Americans cheerfully planted "Victory" vegetable gardens—20 million of them in 1943 alone. With gasoline in short supply, most citizens were limited to 3 gallons (11 liters) a week. The government froze wages and prices and instituted a 48-hour workweek. The economy hummed with war work, rushing out arms and equipment. On assembly lines, housewives and mothers built airplanes, ships, and munitions as husbands and fathers left for the front.

Despite the worry and hardship of the war, life on other fronts yielded some artistic and creative surprises. The landmark musical *Oklahoma!* debuted on Broadway, the first one based on a real story line with serious music and dancing instead of the popular chorus line of glamorous girls. Black actor and singer Paul Robeson gave such a powerful performance as the lead in Shakespeare's *Othello* (a black character) on Broadway, that controversy over his race gave way to acclaim and a record-breaking run. Jazzman Duke Ellington premiered his orchestral suite *Black, Brown, and Beige*, based on a variety of African-American music, at New York's Carnegie Hall. In Hollywood, a little film called *Casablanca* won the Academy Award.

Emerging from the American mix in 1943 was a new creature called the "teenager." Until then, treated as young adults or old children, Americans in their teens were coming into their own as a force to be reckoned with and marketed to with fashion, cosmetics, magazines, and music. No musician quickened the collective heartbeat of America's "bobbysoxers" more than a slender young singer named Frank Sinatra, whose first million-record seller came out in 1943. Girls swooned when Frankie crooned, and the teen idol was born. Also born that year were future idols George Harrison, Janis Joplin, and Mick Jagger.

Americans in 1943 struggled to balance the horrors of war and the joys of ordinary life.

The Presidents and Their First Ladies

YEARS IN OFFICE			
President	Birth–Death	First Lady	Birth–Death
1789–1797			
George Washington	1732–1799	Martha Dandridge Custis Washington	1731–1802
1797–1801			
John Adams	1735–1826	Abigail Smith Adams	1744–1818
1801–1809			
Thomas Jefferson†	1743–1826		
1809–1817			
James Madison	1751–1836	Dolley Payne Todd Madison	1768–1849
1817–1825			
James Monroe	1758–1831	Elizabeth Kortright Monroe	1768–1830
1825–1829			
John Quincy Adams	1767–1848	Louisa Catherine Johnson Adams	1775–1852
1829–1837			
Andrew Jackson†	1767–1845		
1837–1841			
Martin Van Buren†	1782–1862		
1841			
William Henry Harrison‡	1773–1841		
1841–1845			
John Tyler	1790–1862	Letitia Christian Tyler (1841–1842)	1790–1842
		Julia Gardiner Tyler (1844–1845)	1820–1889
1845–1849			
James K. Polk	1795–1849	Sarah Childress Polk	1803–1891
1849–1850			
Zachary Taylor	1784–1850	Margaret Mackall Smith Taylor	1788–1852
1850–1853			
Millard Fillmore	1800–1874	Abigail Powers Fillmore	1798–1853
1853–1857			
Franklin Pierce	1804–1869	Jane Means Appleton Pierce	1806–1863
1857–1861			
James Buchanan*	1791–1868		
1861–1865			
Abraham Lincoln	1809–1865	Mary Todd Lincoln	1818–1882
1865–1869			
Andrew Johnson	1808–1875	Eliza McCardle Johnson	1810–1876
1869–1877			
Ulysses S. Grant	1822–1885	Julia Dent Grant	1826–1902
1877–1881			
Rutherford B. Hayes	1822–1893	Lucy Ware Webb Hayes	1831–1889
1881			
James A. Garfield	1831–1881	Lucretia Rudolph Garfield	1832–1918
1881–1885			
Chester A. Arthur†	1829–1886		

† wife died before he took office   ‡ wife too ill to accompany him to Washington   * never married

1885–1889			
Grover Cleveland	1837–1908	Frances Folsom Cleveland	1864–1947
1889–1893			
Benjamin Harrison	1833–1901	Caroline Lavinia Scott Harrison	1832–1892
1893–1897			
Grover Cleveland	1837–1908	Frances Folsom Cleveland	1864–1947
1897–1901			
William McKinley	1843–1901	Ida Saxton McKinley	1847–1907
1901–1909			
Theodore Roosevelt	1858–1919	Edith Kermit Carow Roosevelt	1861–1948
1909–1913			
William Howard Taft	1857–1930	Helen Herron Taft	1861–1943
1913–1921			
Woodrow Wilson	1856–1924	Ellen Louise Axson Wilson (1913–1914)	1860–1914
		Edith Bolling Galt Wilson (1915–1921)	1872–1961
1921–1923			
Warren G. Harding	1865–1923	Florence Kling Harding	1860–1924
1923–1929			
Calvin Coolidge	1872–1933	Grace Anna Goodhue Coolidge	1879–1957
1929–1933			
Herbert Hoover	1874–1964	Lou Henry Hoover	1874–1944
1933–1945			
Franklin D. Roosevelt	1882–1945	Anna Eleanor Roosevelt	1884–1962
1945–1953			
Harry S. Truman	1884–1972	Bess Wallace Truman	1885–1982
1953–1961			
Dwight D. Eisenhower	1890–1969	Mamie Geneva Doud Eisenhower	1896–1979
1961–1963			
John F. Kennedy	1917–1963	Jacqueline Bouvier Kennedy	1929–1994
1963–1969			
Lyndon B. Johnson	1908–1973	Claudia Taylor (Lady Bird) Johnson	1912–
1969–1974			
Richard Nixon	1913–1994	Patricia Ryan Nixon	1912–1993
1974–1977			
Gerald Ford	1913–	Elizabeth Bloomer Ford	1918–
1977–1981			
James Carter	1924–	Rosalynn Smith Carter	1927–
1981–1989			
Ronald Reagan	1911–	Nancy Davis Reagan	1923–
1989–1993			
George Bush	1924–	Barbara Pierce Bush	1925–
1993–			
William Jefferson Clinton	1946–	Hillary Rodham Clinton	1947–

Helen Herron Taft
Timeline

1861	★	Civil War begins
		Helen Herron is born on June 2
1862	★	Union armies are defeated at the Battles of Second Bull Run and Fredericksburg
		Confederate army is defeated at Antietam
1863	★	Emancipation Proclamation goes into effect
		Confederate forces are defeated at the Battles of Gettysburg and Vicksburg
		President Abraham Lincoln gives the Gettysburg Address
1864	★	Abraham Lincoln is reelected president
1865	★	The Civil War ends
		Abraham Lincoln is assassinated
		Andrew Johnson becomes president
1866	★	Final transatlantic cable is laid between Great Britain and the United States
1868	★	Ulysses S. Grant is elected president
1869	★	National Women Suffrage Association is formed
1871	★	Fire destroys most of Chicago
1872	★	Susan B. Anthony is arrested for trying to vote
		Ulysses S. Grant is reelected president
		Yellowstone National Park becomes the first U.S. national park
1873	★	Economic depression spreads throughout the United States
1876	★	George Armstrong Custer and his troops are killed at the Battle of the Little Big Horn
1877	★	Rutherford B. Hayes becomes president

1879	☆	Women win the right to argue cases before the Supreme Court
1880	☆	James Garfield is elected president
1881	☆	James A. Garfield is shot and dies about three months later
		Chester A. Arthur becomes president
1882	☆	Congress approves a pension for widows of U.S. presidents
1884	☆	Grover Cleveland is elected president
1886	☆	Geronimo surrenders to the U.S. Army
		Helen Herron marries William Howard Taft
		American Federation of Labor is organized
1887	☆	Interstate Commerce Commission is established
1888	☆	Benjamin Harrison is elected president
1889	☆	Flood in Johnstown, Pennsylvania, kills 2,295 people
		Robert Alphonso Taft is born
1891	☆	Populist Party is formed
		Helen Herron Taft is born
1892	☆	Ellis Island immigration center opens
		Grover Cleveland is elected president
1893	☆	Woman suffrage is adopted in Colorado
		Economic depression hits the United States
1895	☆	Cuba begins a revolt against Spain
1896	☆	William McKinley is elected president
		First Ford automobile is built in Detroit

1897	☆	Charles Phelps Taft is born
1898	☆	Spanish-American War is fought, resulting in the United States annexing Puerto Rico, Guam, and the Philippines
1900	☆	William McKinley is reelected president
		William Howard Taft is named president of the second Philippine commission

1901	★	William Howard Taft is appointed governor-general of the Philippines
		President McKinley is assassinated
		Theodore Roosevelt becomes president
1902	★	Cuba wins independence from Spain
1903	★	Panama and the United States sign a treaty for the building of the Panama Canal
1904	★	Theodore Roosevelt is elected president
		William Howard Taft is named secretary of war
1905	★	Russo-Japanese War is fought and President Roosevelt helps negotiate peace
1906	★	Theodore Roosevelt receives the Nobel Peace Prize
1908	★	William Howard Taft is elected president
1909	★	National Association for the Advancement of Colored People (NAACP) is founded
1912	★	*Titanic* sinks in the North Atlantic
		Woodrow Wilson is elected president
1913	★	Henry Ford sets up his first assembly line
1914	★	Panama Canal is completed
		World War I begins
1916	★	Woodrow Wilson is reelected president
		National Park Service is established
1917	★	United States enters World War I
1918	★	United States and its allies win World War I
1920	★	Nineteenth Amendment, which gave women the right to vote, is added to the U.S. Constitution
		Warren G. Harding is elected president
		Woodrow Wilson receives the Nobel Peace Prize for trying to establish a just peace after World War I
1921	★	William Howard Taft is confirmed as chief justice of the U.S. Supreme Court
1922	★	First woman is appointed to the U.S. Senate

1923	★	President Harding dies
		Calvin Coolidge becomes president
1924	★	Calvin Coolidge is elected president
1925	★	William Howard Taft administers the oath of office to President Calvin Coolidge
1927	★	Charles Lindbergh flies solo across the Atlantic Ocean
1928	★	Herbert Hoover is elected president
		Amelia Earhart becomes the first woman to fly across the Atlantic Ocean
1929	★	William Howard Taft administers the oath of office to President Herbert Hoover
		Stock market crashes, which starts the Great Depression
1930	★	William Howard Taft resigns from Supreme Court
		William Howard Taft dies
1932	★	Amelia Earhart becomes the first woman to fly solo across the Atlantic Ocean
		Franklin D. Roosevelt is elected president
1933	★	President Roosevelt launches the New Deal
1935	★	Congress passes the Social Security Act
1936	★	Franklin D. Roosevelt is reelected president
1939	★	World War II begins
1940	★	Franklin D. Roosevelt is reelected president
1941	★	Japanese bomb Pearl Harbor
		United States enters World War II
1942	★	Japanese capture the Philippines
		U.S. forces win Battle of Midway
		U.S. Marines land at Guadalcanal
		U.S. Army lands in North Africa
1943	★	U.S. and British armies invade Italy
		Food rationing begins in the United States
		Helen Herron Taft dies on May 22

Fast Facts about Helen Herron Taft

Born: June 2, 1861, in Cincinnati, Ohio

Died: May 22, 1943, in Washington, D.C.

Burial Site: Arlington National Cemetery, Arlington, Virginia

Parents: Harriet Collins Herron and John Williamson Herron

Education: Graduated from Miss Nourse's School in Cincinnati; attended Miami University (Oxford, Ohio); studied music and took piano lessons

Career: Teacher

Marriage: To William Howard Taft on June 19, 1886, until his death on March 3, 1930

Children: Robert Alphonso Taft, Helen Herron Taft, and Charles Phelps Taft

Places She Lived: Cincinnati, Ohio (1861–1900); the Philippines (1900–1903); Washington, D.C. (1904–1913; 1921–1943); New Haven, Connecticut (1913–1921)

Major Achievements:

* Became the first First Lady to ride in the same carriage with her husband in the Inaugural Parade.
* Became the first First Lady to give her inaugural gown to the First Ladies Collection at the National Museum of American History at the Smithsonian Institution.
* Arranged to have a bandstand built in Potomac Park.
* Arranged for the Japanese government to give 3,000 cherry trees to be planted along the Tidal Basin in Potomac Park (1912).
* Made it possible for people of color to be hired at the White House.
* Became the first First Lady to publish her memoirs, *Recollections of Full Years* (1914).

Fast Facts about
William Howard Taft's Presidency

Term of Office: Elected in 1908; served as the twenty-seventh president of the United States from 1909 to 1913.

Vice President: James Schoolcraft Sherman, March 4, 1909, until his death on October 30, 1912.

Major Policy Decisions and Legislation:

*   Appointed five associate justices to the U.S. Supreme Court: Horace H. Lurton (1910); Charles Evans Hughes, Willis Van Devanter, Joseph Rucker Lamar (1910); and Mahlon Pitney (1912).

*   Signed the Payne-Aldrich Tariff Act (1909), which raised some tariffs, lowered others, and placed an income tax on corporations.

*   Appointed Edward Douglass White as chief justice of the U.S. Supreme Court (1910).

*   Appointed Julia C. Lathrop as director of the federal Children's Bureau, the first woman to be appointed to a major federal post (1912).

*   Proposed an amendment to the U.S. Constitution that would limit the term of office of the president and vice president to one term of six years (1913.)

*   Signed a bill that established the Department of Labor as a separate cabinet post no longer connected to the Department of Commerce (1913).

Major Events:

*   Admiral Peary reached the North Pole (1909).

*   President Taft was the first president to throw out the first baseball to open the baseball season (1910).

*   New Mexico and Arizona became the 47th and 48th states (1912).

*   Parcel post service began (1913).

*   The Sixteenth Amendment, which gave Congress the right to collect income taxes, was added to the U.S. Constitution (1913).

Where to Visit

The Capitol Building
Constitution Avenue
Washington, D.C. 20510
(202) 225-3121

Museum of American History of the
   Smithsonian Institution "First
   Ladies: Political and Public Image"
14th Street and Constitution Avenue
   NW
Washington, D.C.
(202) 357-2008

National Archives
Constitution Avenue
Washington, D.C. 20408
(202) 501-5000

The National First Ladies Library
The Saxton McKinley House
331 South Market Avenue
Canton, Ohio 44702

White House
1600 Pennsylvania Avenue
Washington, D.C. 20500
Visitor's Office: (202) 456-7041

White House Historical Association
740 Jackson Place NW
Washington, D.C. 20503
(202) 737-8292

William Howard Taft National Historic
   Site
2038 Auburn Avenue
Cincinnati, Ohio 45219-3025
Phone: (513) 684-3262
Fax: (513) 684-3627

Online Sites of Interest

The First Ladies of the United States of America
http://www2.whitehouse.gov/WH/glimpse/ firstladies/html/firstladies.html
A portrait and biographical sketch of each First Lady plus links to other White House sites

Internet Public Library, Presidents of the United States (IPL POTUS)
http://www.ipl.org/ref/POTUS/ fdroosevelt.html
An excellent site with much information on William Howard Taft, including personal information and facts about his presidency; many links to other sites including biographies and other Internet resources.

The National First Ladies Library
http://www.firstladies.org
The first virtual library devoted to the lives and legacies of America's First Ladies; includes a bibliography of books, articles, letters, and manuscripts by and about the nation's First Ladies; also includes a virtual tour, with pictures, of the restored Saxton McKinley House in Canton, Ohio, which houses the library.

William Howard Taft National Historic Site
http://www.nps.gov/wiho/
William Howard Taft was born and raised in this home in Cincinnati, Ohio. It is the only memorial to the nation's twenty-seventh president and tenth chief justice, who is buried in Arlington National Cemetery.

The White House
http://www.whitehouse.gov/WH/ Welcome.html
Information about the current president and vice president; White House history and tours; biographies of past presidents and their families; a virtual tour of the historic building; current events; and much more

The White House for Kids
http://www.whitehouse.gov/WH/kids/html/ kidshome.html
This site includes information about White House kids, past and present; famous "First Pets," past and present; historic moments of the presidency; several issues of a newsletter called "Inside the White House"; and more.

For Further Reading

Casey, Jane Clark. *William Howard Taft: Twenty-Seventh President of the United States*. Encyclopedia of Presidents. Chicago: Childrens Press, 1989.

Fradin, Dennis Brindell. *Ohio*. Sea to Shining Sea series. Chicago: Childrens Press, 1993.

Gormley, Beatrice. *First Ladies*. New York: Scholastic, Inc., 1997.

Gould, Lewis L. (ed.). *American First Ladies: Their Lives and Their Legacy*. New York: Garland Publishing, 1996.

Guzzetti, Paula. *The White House*. Parsippany, N.J.: Silver Burdett Press, 1995.

Jacobson, Doranne. *Presidents and First Ladies of the United States*. New York: Smithmark Publishers, Inc., 1995.

Klapthor, Margaret Brown. *The First Ladies*. 8th edition. Washington, D.C.: White House Historical Association, 1995.

Lepthien, Emilie U. *The Philippines*. Danbury, Conn.: Children's Press, 1996.

Mann, Elizabeth. *The Panama Canal: The Story of How a Jungle Was Conquered and the World Made Smaller*. Wonders of the World series. New York: Mikaya Press, 1998.

Mayo, Edith P. (ed.). *The Smithsonian Book of the First Ladies: Their Lives, Times, and Issues*. New York: Henry Holt, 1996.

Sandak, Cass R. *The Tafts*. First Families series. New York: Crestwood House, 1993.

Stewart, Gail B. *World War I*. America's Wars series. San Diego: Lucent Books, 1991.

Index

Page numbers in **boldface type** indicate illustrations

Photo Identifications

Cover: Official White House portrait of Helen Herron Taft by Bror Kronstrand
Page 8: An undated photograph of Helen Herron as a young girl
Page 24: Helen Taft as a young woman
Page 40: An undated photograph of Helen Taft
Page 56: Detail of a portrait of Helen Herron Taft as First Lady by Bror Kronstrand; portrait of President William Howard Taft
Page 70: An undated photograph of First Lady Helen Herron Taft
Page 84: A photograph of former First Lady Helen Herron Taft with her husband, Chief Justice William Howard Taft

Photo Credits©

About the Author

Judith Greenberg has more than 29 years of experience in education and has taught in both public and private schools in Washington, D.C.; Montgomery County, Maryland; Prince Georges County, Maryland; and the state of New Jersey. Her teaching career also includes master teaching and directing 21 grants on various subjects. She is the author and co-author of 37 library books for children and teens. For more than 25 years, Ms. Greenberg has worked with families seeking a better education for their learning-different or brain-injured children. In this capacity, she is the Founder and Director of SchoolFinders, an educational consulting firm in Potomac, Maryland, and Washington, D.C.

Judith Greenberg has written 25,000 test questions (something she hopes never to do again) and curriculum guides and kits. She also provides seminars for parents of "at-risk" students who wish to learn better ways of helping their children through the school process.

As an author, Judith Greenberg has received many national awards, including the coveted *Notable Children's Book* for 1996 for *A Pioneer Woman's Memoirs*, part of the Franklin Watts In Their Own Words series. Currently completing her doctorate in education, Ms. Greenberg is also the education consultant for the Environmental Protection Agency at its headquarters in Washington, D.C.

An avid swimmer and reader of mysteries and historical novels, Ms. Greenberg spends most of her free time with her nearly grown son and daughter and shares her home with a yellow Labrador retriever and a brown and white American Staffordshire terrier. Judith Greenberg hopes you enjoy this book and adds that she loves to get e-mail from readers at: Schoolfind@aol.com.